World Languages

Families in
German

Daniel Nunn

Raintree is an imprint of Capstone Global Library
Limited, a company incorporated in England and Wales
having its registered office at 7 Pilgrim Street, London,
EC4V 6LB – Registered company number: 6695582

To contact Raintree please phone 0845 6044371,
fax + 44 (0) 1865 312263, or email:
myorders@raintreepublishers.co.uk. Customers from
outside the UK please telephone +44 1865 312262.

Edited by Daniel Nunn, Rebecca Rissman & Sian Smith
Designed by Joanna Hinton-Malivoire
Picture research by Tracy Cummins
Production by Victoria Fitzgerald
Originated by Capstone Global Library Ltd
Printed and bound in China by Leo Paper Products Ltd

ISBN 978 1 406 25087 9
16 15 14 13 12
10 9 8 7 6 5 4 3 2 1

British Library Cataloguing in Publication Data
Nunn, Daniel.
Families in German: die Familien. – (World languages.
Families)
1. German language–Vocabulary–Pictorial works–
Juvenile literature. 2. Families–Germany–Terminology–
Pictorial works–Juvenile literature.
I. Title II. Series
  438.1-dc23

Acknowledgements
We would like to thank the following for permission to
reproduce photographs: Shutterstock pp.4 (Catalin
Petolea), 5 (optimarc), 5, 6 (Petrenko Andriy), 5, 7
(Tyler Olson), 5, 8 (Andrey Shadrin), 9 (Erika Cross), 10
(Alena Brozova), 5, 11 (Maxim Petrichuk), 12 (auremar),
13 (Mika Heittola), 5, 14, 15 (Alexander Raths), 5, 16
(Samuel Borges), 17 (Vitalii Nesterchuk), 18 (pat138241),
19 (Fotokostic), 20 (Cheryl Casey), 21 (spotmatik).

Cover photographs of two women and a man
reproduced with permission of Shutterstock (Yuri Arcurs).
Cover photograph of a girl reproduced with permission
of istockphoto (© Sean Lockes). Back cover photograph
of a girl reproduced with permission of Shutterstock
(Erika Cross).

We would like to thank Regina Irwin for her invaluable
help in the preparation of this book.

Every effort has been made to contact copyright holders
of material reproduced in this book. Any omissions will
be rectified in subsequent printings if notice is given to
the publisher.

Contents

Hallo!

Ich heisse Daniel.

My name is Daniel.

Hier ist meine Familie.

This is my family.

Meine Mutter und mein Vater

meine Mutter

Hier ist meine Mutter.

This is my mother.

mein Vater

Hier ist mein Vater.

This is my father.

Mein Bruder und meine Schwester

mein Bruder

Hier ist mein Bruder.

This is my brother.

meine Schwester

Hier ist meine Schwester.

This is my sister.

Meine Stiefmutter und mein Stiefvater

meine Stiefmutter

Hier ist meine Stiefmutter.

This is my step-mother.

mein Stiefvater

Hier ist mein Stiefvater.

This is my step-father.

Mein Stiefbruder und meine Stiefschwester

mein Stiefbruder

Hier ist mein Stiefbruder.

This is my step-brother.

meine Stiefschwester

Hier ist meine Stiefschwester.

This is my step-sister.

Meine Grossmutter und mein Grossvater

meine Grossmutter

Hier ist meine Grossmutter.

This is my grandmother.

mein Grossvater

Hier ist mein Grossvater.

This is my grandfather.

Meine Tante und mein Onkel

meine Tante

Hier ist meine Tante.

This is my aunt.

mein Onkel

Hier ist mein Onkel.

This is my uncle.

Meine Cousine und mein Cousin

meine Cousine

Hier sind meine Cousine und
mein Cousin.

(18) These are my cousins.

mein Cousin

19

Meine Freunde

meine Freundin

Hier sind meine Freunde.

These are my friends.

21

Dictionary

German word	How to say it	English word
Bruder	broo-dah	brother
Cousin	koo-sang	cousin (male)
Cousine	koo-see-nah	cousin (female)
Familie	fam-eel-ee-ya	family
Freund	froind	friend (male)
Freunde	froin-dah	friends
Freundin	froin-din	friend (female)
Grossmutter	groas-moo-tah	grandmother
Grossvater	groas-fah-tah	grandfather
hallo	hal-oh	hi
Hier ist / Hier sind	hear isst / hear sinned	This is / These are
Ich heisse	ik high-sah	My name is
mein	mine	my (male)
meine	min-ah	my (female)
meine	min-ah	my (plural)

22

German word	How to say it	English word
Mutter	moo-tah	mother
Onkel	on-kal	uncle
Schwester	shwess-tah	sister
Stiefbruder	shteef-broo-dah	step-brother
Stiefmutter	shteef-moo-tah	step-mother
Stiefschwester	shteef-shwess-tah	step-sister
Stiefvater	shteef-fah-tah	step-father
Tante	tan-tah	aunt
und	oond	and
Vater	fah-tah	father

See words in the "How to say it" columns for a rough guide to pronunciations.

Index

Notes for parents and teachers

In German, nouns always begin with a capital letter.

The spelling of the German word for "my" changes depending on whether it is masculine, feminine, or plural.